The
Neighborhood
SING-
ALONG

For Asa

The Neighborhood SING-ALONG

By Nina Crews

Greenwillow Books, *An Imprint of HarperCollinsPublishers*

Contents

If You're Happy and You Know It .6

Do Your Ears Hang Low? .8

Skip to My Lou .10

The Wheels on the Bus .12

Hush, Little Baby .14

The Alphabet Song .16

Frère Jacques .18

Oh, Little Playmate .19

I've Been Working on the Railroad .21

I'm a Little Teapot .22

One, Two, Buckle My Shoe .23

This Little Light of Mine .25

Take Me Out to the Ball Game! .26

La Bamba .28

There's a Hole in the Bucket .30

Sailing, Sailing .32

Row, Row, Row Your Boat .33

Oh Where, Oh Where Has My Little Dog Gone? .34

The Animal Fair .36

A-Tisket, A-Tasket .38

Miss Lucy .40

It's Raining, It's Pouring .42

Here We Go Round the Mulberry Bush .44

Mary Had a Little Lamb .45

Short'nin' Bread .46

Miss Mary Mack .48

Alexander's Ragtime Band .50

John Jacob Jingleheimer Schmidt .52

Shoo, Fly! .53

London Bridge Is Falling Down .54

Oh, Dear, What Can the Matter Be? .56

Alouette .59

Down by the Riverside .60

Yankee Doodle .63

If You're Happy and You Know It

If you're happy and you know it,
Clap your hands.
If you're happy and you know it,
Clap your hands.
If you're happy and you know it,
Then your face will surely show it,
If you're happy and you know it,
Clap your hands.

If you're happy and you know it,
Stomp your feet.
If you're happy and you know it,
Stomp your feet.
If you're happy and you know it,
Then your face will surely show it,
If you're happy and you know it,
Stomp your feet.

If you're happy and you know it,
Shout "Hurray!"
If you're happy and you know it,
Shout "Hurray!"
If you're happy and you know it,
Then your face will surely show it,
If you're happy and you know it,
Shout "Hurray!"

7

Do Your Ears Hang Low?

Do your ears hang low?
Do they wobble to and fro?
Can you tie them in a knot?
Can you tie them in a bow?
Can you throw them
    o'er your shoulder
Like a Continental soldier?
Do your ears hang low?

Do your ears hang high?
Do they reach up to the sky?
Do they droop when they are wet?
Do they stiffen when they're dry?
Can you semaphore your neighbor
With a minimum of labor?
Do your ears hang high?

Do your ears flip-flop?
Can you use them for a mop?
Are they stringy at the bottom?
Are they curly at the top?
Can you use them for a swatter?
Can you use them for a blotter?
Do your ears flip-flop?

Do your ears hang out?
Can you waggle them about?
Can you flip them up and down
As you fly around the town?
Can you shut them up for sure
When you hear an awful bore?
Do your ears hang out?

Skip to My Lou

Chorus:
Skip, skip, skip to my Lou,
Skip, skip, skip to my Lou,
Skip, skip, skip to my Lou,
Skip to my Lou, my darlin'.

Fly's in the buttermilk,
Shoo, fly, shoo,
Fly's in the buttermilk,
Shoo, fly, shoo,
Fly's in the buttermilk,
Shoo, fly, shoo,
Skip to my Lou, my darlin'.

(chorus)

Off to Texas,
Two by two,
Off to Texas,
Two by two,
Off to Texas,
Two by two,
Skip to my Lou, my darlin'.

(chorus)

The Wheels on the Bus

The wheels on the bus go round and round.
Round and round. Round and round.
The wheels on the bus go round and round,
All through the town.

The driver on the bus says, "Move on back.
Move on back. Move on back."
The driver on the bus says, "Move on back."
All through the town.

The horn on the bus goes *beep, beep, beep.*
Beep, beep, beep. Beep, beep, beep.
The horn on the bus goes *beep, beep, beep,*
All through the town.

The baby on the bus says, "Wah, wah, wah.
Wah, wah, wah. Wah, wah, wah."
The baby on the bus says, "Wah, wah, wah,"
All through the town.

The mommy on the bus says, "Shh, shh, shh.
Shh, shh, shh. Shh, shh, shh."
The mommy on the bus says, "Shh, shh, shh,"
All through the town.

13

Hush, Little Baby

Hush, little baby, don't say a word,
Mama's gonna buy you a mockingbird.

And if that mockingbird won't sing,
Mama's gonna buy you a diamond ring.

And if that diamond ring turns brass,
Mama's gonna buy you a looking glass.

And if that looking glass gets broke,
Mama's gonna buy you a billy goat.

And if that billy goat won't pull,
Mama's gonna buy you a cart and bull.

And if that cart and bull turn over,
Mama's going to buy you a dog named Rover.

And if that dog named Rover won't bark,
Mama's going to buy you a horse and cart.

And if that horse and cart fall down,
You'll still be the sweetest little baby in town.

15

The Alphabet Song

A, B, C, D, E, F, G,

H, I, J, K, L, M, N, O, P,

Q, R, S,

T, U, V,

W, X, Y, and Z.

Now I know my A, B, C's,

Next time won't you sing with me?

Frère Jacques

Frère Jacques, Frère Jacques,
Dormez vous? Dormez vous?
Sonnez les matines,
Sonnez les matines,
Ding ding dong. Ding ding dong.

Are you sleeping, are you sleeping?
Brother John? Brother John?
Morning bells are ringing,
Morning bells are ringing,
Ding ding dong. Ding ding dong.

Oh, Little Playmate

Oh, little playmate,
Come out and play with me,
And bring your dollies three.
Climb up my apple tree,
Holler down my rain barrel,
Slide down my cellar door,
And we'll be jolly friends,
Forever more.

Oh, no, my playmate,
I can't come play with you.
My dollies have the flu,
Boo hoo, boo hoo, boo hoo.
Can't holler down rain barrels,
Or slide down a cellar door,
But we'll be jolly friends,
Forever more.

I've Been Working on the Railroad

I've been working on the railroad,
All the livelong day.
I've been working on the railroad,
Just to pass the time away.
Can't you hear the whistle blowing,
Rise up so early in the morn,
Can't you hear the captain shouting,
"Dinah, blow your horn!"

Dinah, won't you blow,
Dinah, won't you blow,
Dinah, won't you blow your horn?
Dinah, won't you blow,
Dinah, won't you blow,
Dinah, won't you blow your horn?

Someone's in the kitchen with Dinah,
Someone's in the kitchen I know.
Someone's in the kitchen with Dinah,
Strumming on the old banjo,
Singing,

Fee, fie, fiddle-e-o,
Fee, fie, fiddle-e-o,
Fee, fie, fiddle-e-o,
Strumming on the old banjo.

I'm a Little Teapot

I'm a little teapot, short and stout,
Here is my handle, here is my spout,
When I get all steamed up, hear me shout,
Just tip me over and pour me out!

One, Two, Buckle My Shoe

One, two, buckle my shoe,
Three, four, shut the door,
Five, six, pick up sticks,
Seven, eight, lay them straight,
Nine, ten, a good fat hen,
Eleven, twelve, dig and delve,
Thirteen, fourteen, maids are courting,
Fifteen, sixteen, maids in the kitchen,
Seventeen, eighteen, maids are waiting,
Nineteen, twenty, my platter's empty.

This Little Light of Mine

This little light of mine,
I'm going to let it shine,
Oh, this little light of mine,
I'm going to let it shine,
This little light of mine,
I'm going to let it shine,
Let it shine, let it shine,
    let it shine.

Everywhere I go,
I'm going to let it shine,
Oh, everywhere I go,
I'm going to let it shine,
Everywhere I go,
I'm going to let it shine,
Let it shine, let it shine,
    let it shine.

I'm not going to make it shine,
I'm just going to let it shine,
I'm not going to make it shine,
I'm just going to let it shine,
I'm not going to make it shine,
I'm just going to let it shine,
Let it shine, let it shine,
    let it shine.

Out in the dark,
I'm going to let it shine,
Oh, out in the dark,
I'm going to let it shine,
Out in the dark,
I'm going to let it shine,
Let it shine, let it shine,
    let it shine.

Take Me Out
to the Ball Game!

Take me out to the ball game,
Take me out with the crowd;
Buy me some peanuts and Cracker Jack,
I don't care if I never get back.

Let me root, root, root for the home team,
If they don't win, it's a shame.
For it's one, two, three strikes, you're out,
At the old ball game.

La Bamba

Para bailar la Bamba,
Para bailar la Bamba,
se necesita una poca de gracia.
Una poca de gracia, y otra cosita

Y arriba, y arriba, y arriba iré
Por ti seré, por ti seré.

Chorus:
Bamba, bamba. Bamba, bamba. Bamba, bamba.

Yo no soy marinero. Yo no soy marinero.
Soy capitán, soy capitán.

(chorus)

29

There's a Hole in the Bucket

There's a hole in the bucket, dear Liza, dear Liza,
There's a hole in the bucket, dear Liza, a hole.

So fix it, dear Henry, dear Henry, dear Henry,
So fix it, dear Henry, dear Henry, fix it.

With what should I fix it, dear Liza, dear Liza,
With what should I fix it, dear Liza, with what?

With straw, dear Henry, dear Henry, dear Henry,
With straw, dear Henry, dear Henry, with straw.

But the straw is too long, dear Liza, dear Liza,
The straw is too long, dear Liza, too long.

So cut it, dear Henry, dear Henry, dear Henry,
So cut it, dear Henry, dear Henry, cut it!

With what should I cut it, dear Liza, dear Liza,
With what should I cut it, dear Liza, with what?

With a knife, dear Henry, dear Henry, dear Henry,
With a knife, dear Henry, dear Henry, a knife.

But the knife's too dull, dear Liza, dear Liza,
The knife's too dull, dear Liza, too dull.

So sharpen it, dear Henry, dear Henry, dear Henry,
So sharpen it, dear Henry, dear Henry, sharpen it!

With what should I sharpen it, dear Liza, dear Liza,
With what should I sharpen it, dear Liza, with what?

Use the stone, dear Henry, dear Henry, dear Henry,
Use the stone, dear Henry, dear Henry, the stone.

But the stone is too dry, dear Liza, dear Liza,
The stone is too dry, dear Liza, too dry.

So wet it, dear Henry, dear Henry, dear Henry,
So wet it, dear Henry, dear Henry, wet it.

With what should I wet it, dear Liza, dear Liza,
With what should I wet it, dear Liza, with what?

With water, dear Henry, dear Henry, dear Henry,
With water, dear Henry, dear Henry, with water.

With what should I carry it, dear Liza, dear Liza,
With what should I carry it, dear Liza, with what?

Use the bucket, dear Henry, dear Henry, dear Henry,
Use the bucket, dear Henry, dear Henry, the bucket!

There's a hole in the bucket, dear Liza, dear Liza,
There's a hole in the bucket, dear Liza, a hole.

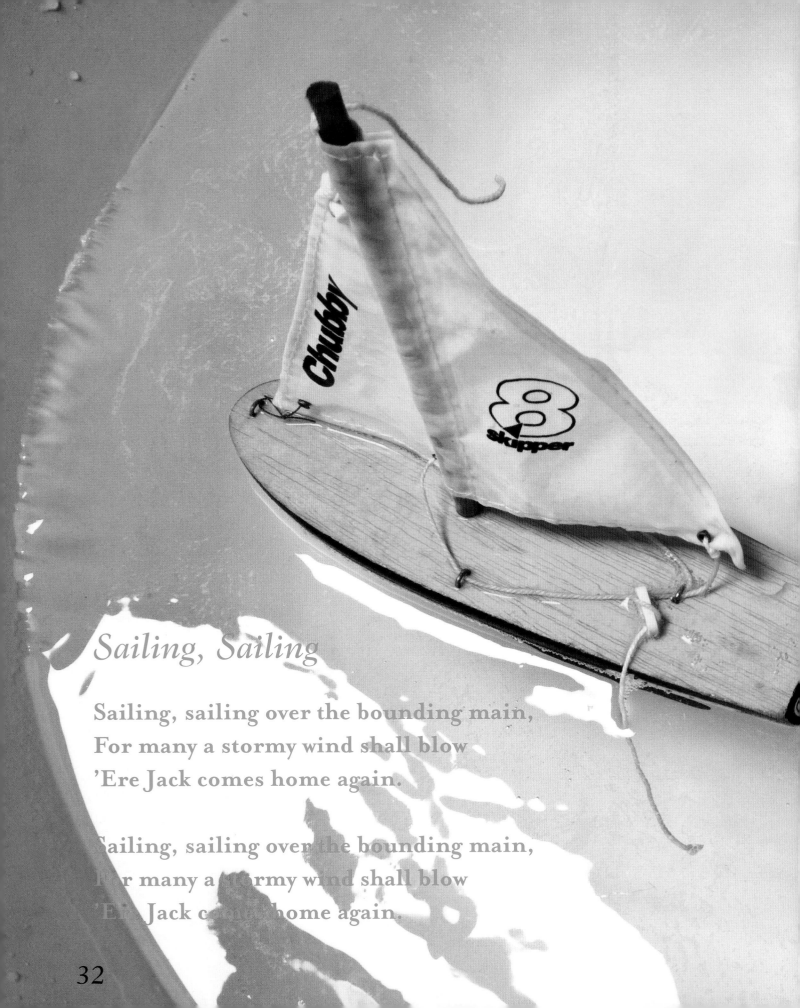

Sailing, Sailing

Sailing, sailing over the bounding main,
For many a stormy wind shall blow
'Ere Jack comes home again.

Sailing, sailing over the bounding main,
For many a stormy wind shall blow
'Ere Jack comes home again.

Row, Row, Row Your Boat

Row, row, row your boat,
Gently down the stream.
Merrily, merrily, merrily, merrily,
Life is but a dream.

Oh Where, Oh Where
Has My Little Dog Gone?

Oh where, oh where has my little dog gone?
Oh where, oh where can he be?
With his ears cut short and his tail cut long,
Oh where, oh where can he be?

The Animal Fair

I went to the Animal Fair,
The birds and the beasts were there,
The big baboon by the light of the moon,
Was combing his auburn hair.

The monkey fell out of his bunk,
Slid down the elephant's trunk,
The elephant sneezed and fell on his knees,
And what became of the monk, the monk . . .

36

A-Tisket, A-Tasket

A-tisket, a-tasket,
A green and yellow basket.
I wrote a letter to my love,
And on the way I dropped it.

I dropped it, I dropped it,
Yes, on the way I dropped it,
A little girlie picked it up,
And took it to the market.

38

She was truckin' on down the avenue,
Without a single thing to do,
She was peck, peck, peckin' all around,
When she spied it on the ground.

A-tisket, a-tasket,
She took my yellow basket.
And if she doesn't bring it back,
I think that I shall die.

(Was it red?) No, no, no, no.
(Was it brown?) No, no, no, no.
(Was it blue?) No, no, no, no.
Just a little yellow basket.

39

Miss Lucy

Miss Lucy had a baby,
She named him Tiny Tim.
She put him in the bathtub,
To see if he could swim.

He drank up all the water,
He ate up all the soap,
He tried to eat the bathtub,
But it wouldn't go down his throat.

Miss Lucy called the doctor,
Miss Lucy called the nurse,
Miss Lucy called the lady
With the alligator purse.

"Chicken pox!" said the doctor,
"Measles!" said the nurse,
"Mumps!" said the lady
With the alligator purse.

Out walked the doctor,
Out walked the nurse,
Out walked the lady
With the alligator purse.

It's Raining, It's Pouring

It's raining, it's pouring,
The old man is snoring.
He went to bed
And he bumped his head
And he couldn't get up
In the morning.

42

Here We Go Round
the Mulberry Bush

Here we go round the mulberry bush,
The mulberry bush, the mulberry bush.
Here we go round the mulberry bush.
So early in the morning.

This is the way we wash our face,
Wash our face, wash our face.
This is the way we wash our face,
So early in the morning.

This is the way we go to school,
Go to school, go to school.
This is the way we go to school,
So early in the morning.

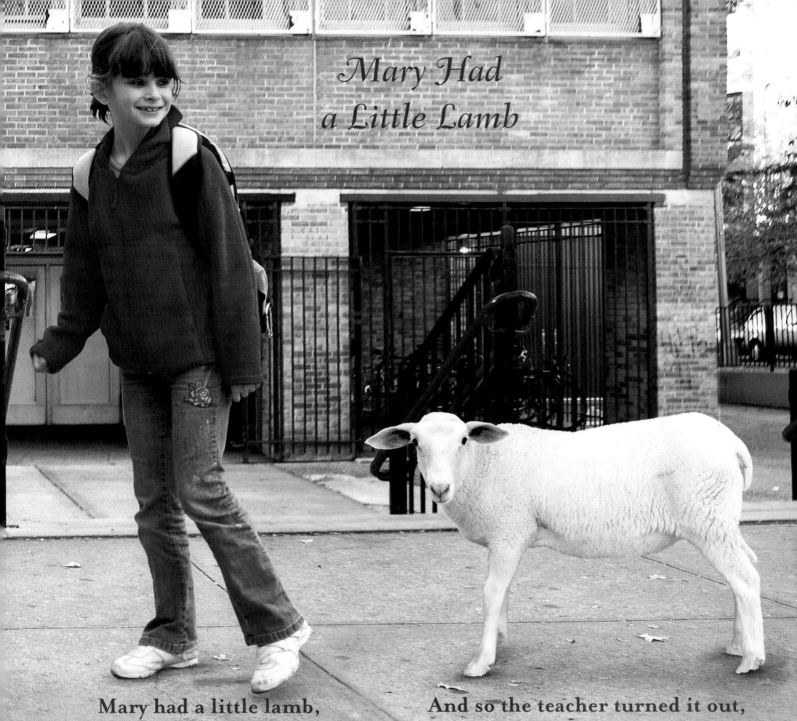

Mary Had a Little Lamb

Mary had a little lamb,
Its fleece was white as snow;
And everywhere that Mary went
The lamb was sure to go.

It followed her to school one day,
That was against the rules;
It made the children laugh and play
To see a lamb at school.

And so the teacher turned it out,
But still it lingered near;
And waited patiently about
Till Mary did appear.

Why does the lamb love Mary so?
The eager children cry;
Why, Mary loves the lamb, you know,
The teacher did reply.

Short'nin' Bread

Put on the skillet, slip on the lid,
Mama's gonna make a little short'nin' bread.
That ain't all she's gonna do,
Mama's gonna make a little coffee, too.

Chorus:
Mama's little baby loves short'nin', short'nin',
Mama's little baby loves short'nin' bread.
Mama's little baby loves short'nin', short'nin',
Mama's little baby loves short'nin' bread.

Three little children, lyin' in bed
Two were sick and the other 'most dead.
Sent for the doctor and the doctor said,
"Give those children some short'nin' bread."

(chorus)

When those children, sick in bed,
Heard that talk about short'nin' bread,
Popped up well to dance and sing,
Skipped around and cut the pigeon wing.

(chorus)

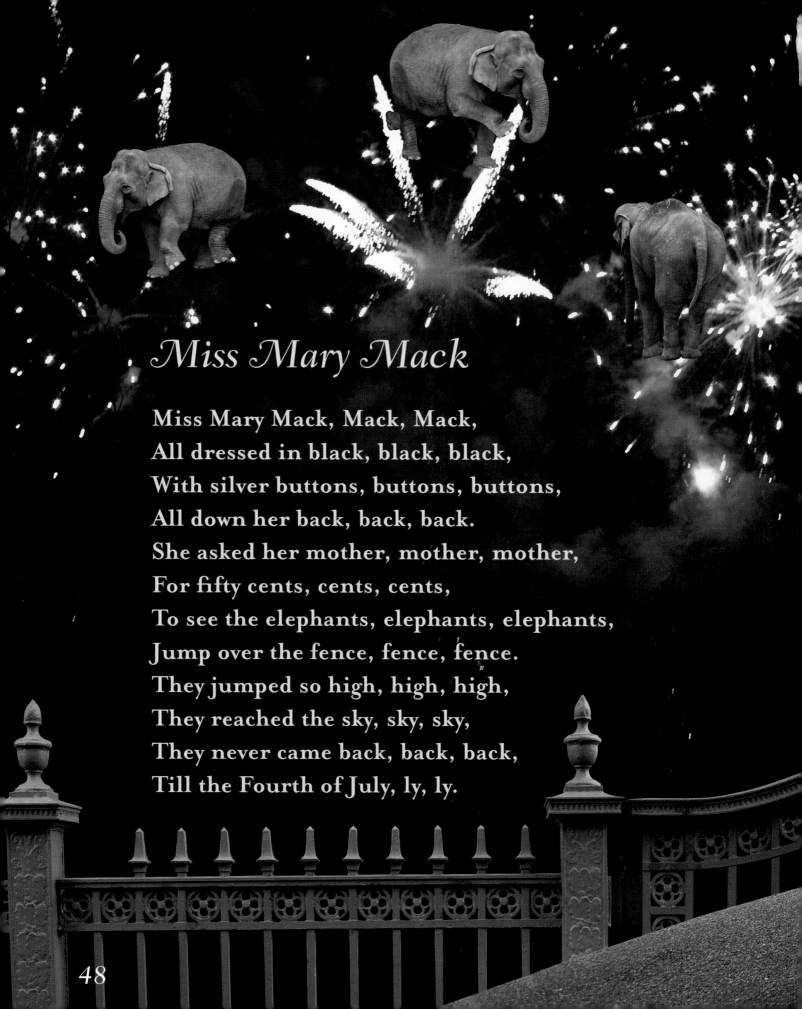

Miss Mary Mack

Miss Mary Mack, Mack, Mack,
All dressed in black, black, black,
With silver buttons, buttons, buttons,
All down her back, back, back.
She asked her mother, mother, mother,
For fifty cents, cents, cents,
To see the elephants, elephants, elephants,
Jump over the fence, fence, fence.
They jumped so high, high, high,
They reached the sky, sky, sky,
They never came back, back, back,
Till the Fourth of July, ly, ly.

Alexander's Ragtime Band

Come on and hear,
Come on and hear,
Alexander's Ragtime Band.
Come on and hear,
Come on and hear,
It's the best band in the land.
They can play a bugle call
Like you never heard before,
So natural that you want to go to war
That's just the bestest band what am,
Honey lamb!

Come on along,
Come on along,
Let me take you by the hand.
Up to the man,
Up to the man,
Who's the leader of the band.
And if you want to hear
The Swanee River played in ragtime
Come on and hear,
Come on and hear,
Alexander's Ragtime Band.

51

John Jacob Jingleheimer Schmidt

John Jacob Jingleheimer Schmidt,
His name is my name, too.
Whenever we go out,
The people always shout,
"There goes John Jacob Jingleheimer Schmidt!"
Da da da da da da da.

Shoo, Fly!

Shoo, fly, don't bother me,
Shoo, fly, don't bother me,
Shoo, fly, don't bother me,
For I belong to somebody.
I feel, I feel,
I feel like a morning star,
I feel, I feel,
I feel like a morning star.

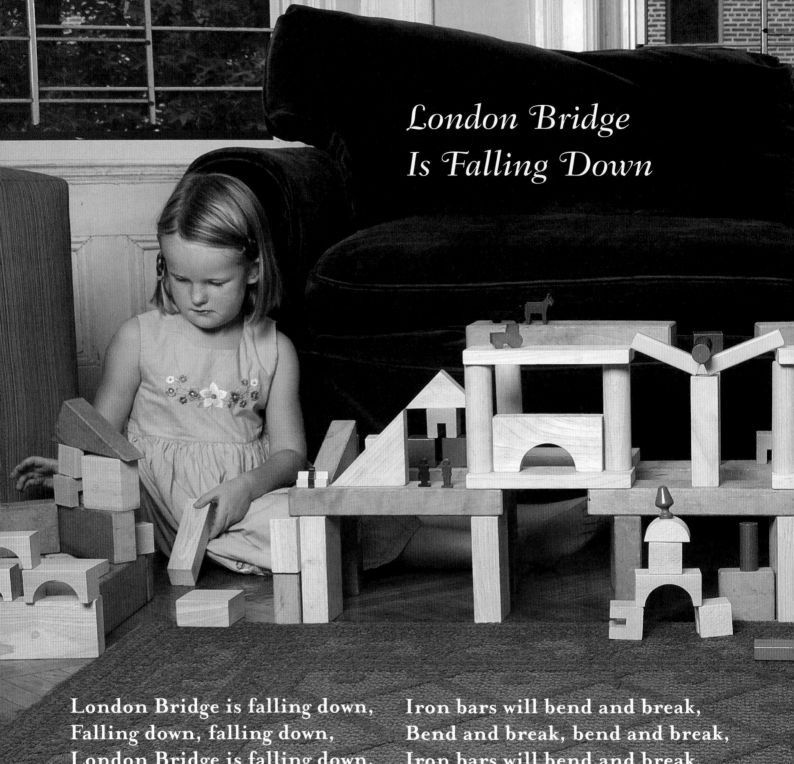

London Bridge Is Falling Down

London Bridge is falling down,
Falling down, falling down,
London Bridge is falling down,
My fair lady!

Build it up with iron bars,
Iron bars, iron bars,
Build it up with iron bars,
My fair lady!

Iron bars will bend and break,
Bend and break, bend and break,
Iron bars will bend and break,
My fair lady!

Build it up with needles and pins,
Needles and pins, needles and pins,
Build it up with needles and pins,
My fair lady!

Pins and needles rust and bend,
Rust and bend, rust and bend,
Pins and needles rust and bend,
My fair lady!

Build it up with silver and gold,
Silver and gold, silver and gold,
Build it up with silver and gold,
My fair lady!

Gold and silver I've not got,
I've not got, I've not got.
Gold and silver I've not got,
My fair lady!

London Bridge is falling down,
Falling down, falling down.
London Bridge is falling down,
My fair lady!

Oh, Dear, What Can the Matter Be?

Oh, dear, what can the matter be?
Dear, dear, what can the matter be?
Oh, dear, what can the matter be?
Johnny's so long at the fair.

He promised to buy me a trinket to please me,
And then for a smile, oh, he vowed he would tease me.
He promised to buy me a bunch of blue ribbons
To tie up my bonny brown hair.

Oh, dear, what can the matter be?
Oh, dear, what can the matter be?
Oh, dear, what can the matter be?
Johnny's so long at the fair.

Alouette

Alouette, gentille Alouette,
Alouette je te plumerai.
Alouette, gentille Alouette,
Alouette je te plumerai.
Je te plumerai la tête,
Je te plumerai la tête,
Et la tête, et la tête,
Alouette, Alouette,
O-o-o-o-oh
Alouette, gentille Alouette,
Alouette je te plumerai.

Gonna lay down my sword and shield, down by the riverside.
Down by the riverside, down by the riverside.
Gonna lay down my sword and shield, down by the riverside.
Ain't gonna study war no more.

Chorus:
I ain't gonna study war no more.
I ain't gonna study war no more.
I ain't gonna study war no more.

I'm gonna lay down my heavy load, down by the riverside,
Down by the riverside, down by the riverside.
I'm gonna lay down my heavy load, down by the riverside.
Ain't gonna study war no more.
(chorus)

I'm gonna lay down my travelin' shoes, down by the riverside,
Down by the riverside, down by the riverside.
I'm gonna lay down my travelin' shoes, down by the riverside.
Ain't gonna study war no more.
(chorus)

Yankee Doodle

Yankee Doodle came to town,
Riding on a pony,
Stuck a feather in his hat,
And called it macaroni.

Yankee Doodle keep it up,
Yankee Doodle dandy,
Mind the music and the step,
And with the girls be handy.

Father and I went down to camp,
Along with Cap'n Gooding,
The men and boys all stood around
As thick as hasty puddin'.

Yankee Doodle keep it up,
Yankee Doodle dandy,
Mind the music and the step,
And with the girls be handy.

Library of Congress Cataloging-in-Publication Data: Crews, Nina. The Neighborhood Sing-Along / by Nina Crews.
p. cm. "Greenwillow Books."
Summary: A collection of songs, both familiar and lesser known, illustrated with photographs in a city setting.
ISBN 978-0-06-185063-9 (trade bdg.)
1. Children's songs, English—Texts. [1. Songs.] I. Title. PZ8.3.C868Ne 2011   782.42—dc22 [E]   2010010340

11 12 13 14 15 SCP 10 9 8 7 6 5 4 3 2 1   First Edition

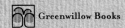 Greenwillow Books

Thank you to everyone who modeled for this book: Asa Antoine, Edward Antoine, Khalil D. Barrera, Kiara R. Barrera, Osarumen Bey, Thandiwe Bey, Adam Bogosian, Ché Campbell, Hazel Lloyd, Derek Catley Jr., Benjamin Chang, Elliott Chang, Jeremy Dorval-Moller, Jackson Ferguson, Owen Ferguson, Susanna Ferguson, Lucia Fishel, Maeve Fishel, Leina Goldman, Charles Jacob-Macias, Maryann Jacob-Macias, Hailey Jurenko, Isabel Keener, Tierra Aili Kobayashi, Max Kumar, Sam Lapp, Odile Lax-Henriques, Zachary Littlejohn, Zoe MacIntyre, Ishai Melamede, Ava Melendez, Raphael Menzer, Sophia Menzer, Anna Kim, Gus Rader, Hazel Rader, Jack Rader, Amy Crews, Chelsea Sánchez, Oliver Schiller-Chubb, Clare Topping, Nora Ward, Jackson-Leroi Widoff-Woodson, Toshi Widoff-Woodson.

Thank you also to Liz Phillips and PS 321; to Rosie, the not-so-lost dog, and Sarah Pirozek; and to the many parents who helped behind the scenes.

This collection includes folk songs, spirituals, nursery rhymes, and pop tunes from the eighteenth, nineteenth, and early twentieth centuries that delight us to this day. In researching this collection, many sources were used—Ronald Herder's *500 Best-Loved Song Lyrics* (Dover Publications, 1998); William and Ceil Baring-Gould's *The Annotated Mother Goose* (Random House, 1981); Carl Sandburg's *The American Songbag* (Harcourt Brace & Company, 1990); online resources, including The Lester S. Levy Collection of Sheet Music (http://levysheetmusic.mse.jhu.edu); and a number of public domain song collections. If you'd like a little help with the tunes, many can be found online at http://kids.niehs.nih.gov/music.htm#index, which hosts MIDI files and song lyrics. And please let this book be only a starting point for sharing these songs and rhymes with your children: some songs have verses not included here, some are great for improvising, and all can be sung, danced, and recited at home, on the bus, at the beach, at the zoo, and all through the town!